PASCALE NAESSENS

Natural food
THAT MAKES YOU HAPPY

LANNOO

Contents

The power of healthy food
Kris Verburgh

Healthy food works like medicine. When people eat more healthily, they can throw 80% of their medication in the trashcan. These are often blood pressure reducers, antacid remedies, anti-inflammatory drugs, blood sugar regulators, etc. It is even possible to postpone the need for some surgical procedures. Researchers at Harvard University investigated a number of patients on a waiting list for heart surgery. Instead of undergoing surgery, they were put on a healthy diet. Within months, 80% of these patients had been removed from the waiting list. In other words, they no longer needed an operation thanks to their conversion to healthy eating. Similar research has also shown that patients who are systematically guided towards healthy eating are ten times less likely to have a heart attack than patients who are treated in a standard manner.

Or take diabetes, a 'chronic' illness that affects 40% of all Europeans at one time or another. A study by the University of Newcastle in England has revealed that diabetes can be a 'reversible' condition. Type-2 diabetes patients were put on a special diet (no bread, potatoes, pasta or rice, and mainly vegetables instead). The results were amazing: in just 8 weeks their diabetes had completely disappeared.

These and many other studies demonstrate the power of healthy food. But it is important that the change in dietary habits should be sufficiently drastic to have the desired effect. These changes need to go much further than the standard recommendations of the government or even of many hospitals. The scientific literature tells us that the healthiest diets are diets with a low glycemic index. These diets are based on foodstuffs that do not cause high blood sugar spikes. Sugar spikes accelerate the ageing process and increase the likelihood of age-related illnesses, such as coronary disease, diabetes and dementia. This means that we all need to eat less bread, potatoes, pasta and rice. These are foodstuffs that consist primarily of starch, and starch is a hidden sugar. Turning these scientific insights into daily practice requires a different kind of eating. Fortunately, this cookbook can offer readers plenty of excellent advice. It is a wonderful book with numerous recipes that are not only healthy, but also make it crystal-clear that healthy eating can also be deliciously tasty. Pure enjoyment, in fact.

KRIS VERBURGH is a doctor and author of the bestselling *The Food Hourglass - stay younger for longer and lose weight.*

Her books reflect her personality

Paul Jambers

"Don't do it!" I begged her. "Please don't start a restaurant." Pascale stood opposite me, proudly holding her recently acquired diploma as a restaurateur. I feared that the next step would be to open her own restaurant. I could already see it: 'Chez Pascale'! Because I know that when Pascale wants to do something, she is a very difficult lady to stop. But a restaurant? No. Never.

For a time, she said nothing more about her plans. I saw, of course, that she was continuing to deepen her knowledge of the art of cooking. I also saw that she spent long evenings studying. Usually scientific books about food and diet. She devoured volume after volume, almost literally. She made notes. She contacted professors and leading dieticians. She followed various courses: healthy living habits, shiatsu and tai chi. At the same time, she took part in workshops organized by famous cooks. I let her do her own thing, but began secretly to hope that she had dropped the restaurant idea. Thankfully, 'Chez Pascale' never opened its doors. Instead, we had 3 books. They are now amongst the bestselling cookbooks in Belgium.

Pascale's books are not just a flash in the pan, nor are they celebrity cookbooks, where a whole team of specialists and assistants actually dream up the recipes, with the role of the 'famous face' being limited to posing behind a cooker in the kitchen for the photographs. Nor does Pascale have a cooking program on television, which often produces these cooking books as a 'spin-off'. No, she has none of that. The secret of her success is very simple: Pascale's books reflect her personality. She does everything herself. She develops the recipes. She goes to the market to buy the ingredients. For the photo shoots, she cooks the meals herself. She directs the photographer. She does the styling. Of course, she writes all the texts as well. And last but not least, she compiles the layout of the book, page by page. But more important than all this, and the real reason for her success, is the fact that Pascale loves her readers. She wants to make people happier and the world a more beautiful place.

PAUL JAMBERS, TV-producer and husband of Pascale Naessens

Food that makes you happy
- simple
- tasty
- healthy
- attractive

Pure Enjoyment is about much more than just cooking. It is about romance, communication, creativity, health and - above all - enjoyment.

It is not perhaps the art of cooking itself that makes this concept so attractive, but rather what you can achieve with it: your most wonderful and most unforgettable moments are often the moments you spend at your own table - and that is the reason why I do what I do. I want to enjoy as many of those super-moments as I possibly can. What's more, I also find great satisfaction and great freedom of expression in creating the right atmosphere, the atmosphere that makes these exceptional moments possible.

It is my way of withdrawing into a special world, a world filled with the people I love: my husband, my friends, my family. It is a world that I consciously wish to make more beautiful, a world that I am happy to be in. I create a setting in which all the different senses are stimulated. The elegance of the table, the romance of being together, the pleasure of delicious food, the freedom of good health... that is what I call pure enjoyment!

It gives a very special feeling to create your own world, and it really is very easy. All you need to do is try.

For many people it is liberating

I had never thought that my books would have such an effect. I was touched in particular by the grateful reactions from so many readers, and this continues to be my strongest motivation for carrying on with my work. It is about people who, after years of searching, have finally found a way of eating that gives them satisfaction. At last, they can both eat and enjoy! They write to tell me that they now have more energy, that their food tastes better than ever before and, above all, that they are healthier and no longer need to battle against those excess pounds. For many people this is liberating, an act of empowerment. All I can say is that my recipes are a simple and natural way of eating, and certainly not a diet! What's more, you can start straight away.

I have not only tried to explain my way of eating as clearly as possible, but also to back it up with scientific evidence. Because that is where much of my inspiration comes from: the professional and scientific literature. Of course, you can just start cooking and ignore all the theory. Because every recipe in this book conforms to that theory, whether you are aware of it or not. Either way, you will soon experience the pleasure and the benefits of healthy eating. You will feel fitter and might even lose weight - whilst at the same time enjoying your food more than ever before.

I have put a great deal of love into this book. It is a reflection of the way I eat and live. I have created the recipes myself and they have been 'tested' (with great pleasure!) by my husband and my friends. Making a book in this very personal manner is an intense process, but I couldn't do it any other way. Yes, it is my passion, and I hope that you can feel that passion and taste it in the recipes. Enjoy!

With best wishes.

Pascale Naessens

Advantages

Making good food combinations is the simplest way to ensure that you eat healthily.

Health
- You feel fitter and don't have that bloated feeling;
- It has a slimming effect;
- You eat more vegetables;
- You eat much fewer (unhealthy) fast carbohydrates (pasta, potatoes, rice, etc.).

It gives you something stable to hold on to in a world of excess.

The most important rule: never combine proteins with carbohydrates.

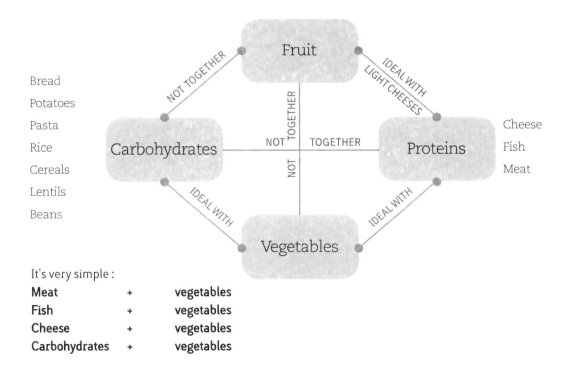

Bread
Potatoes
Pasta
Rice
Cereals
Lentils
Beans

Cheese
Fish
Meat

It's very simple :

Meat	**+**	**vegetables**
Fish	**+**	**vegetables**
Cheese	**+**	**vegetables**
Carbohydrates	**+**	**vegetables**

In practice, this means that you leave the potatoes in the larder and opt for fish or meat with just vegetables.

Health and stability

You feel fitter and don't have that bloated feeling

By making good food combinations, you can digest your meals more easily, so that your body can absorb all the beneficial nutrients. You feel fitter and have more energy.

It has a slimming effect

- Well-digested food stimulates the metabolism.
- You eat far fewer fattening fast carbohydrates.
- The combination of protein + vegetables is the most filling.

Food that is badly digested is more quickly converted into fat. Or rather, the other way around. Food that is well digested stimulates the metabolism, makes you more energetic and, ultimately, slimmer. In particular, it is the fast carbohydrates that make you fatter and encourage food addiction. But by making the right food combinations, you will automatically eat far fewer fast carbohydrates.

And perhaps the most important thing to remember: the combination of protein + vegetables gives you the most satisfied, full feeling. Your desire for 'more food' will fade away.

Protein and fat give you a full feeling as soon as they reach your stomach and small intestine. In contrast, carbohydrates must first be digested and must increase your blood sugar levels before a signal can be sent to your brain to let it know that food has been ingested. It is only then that carbohydrates give you a feeling of being satiated.[2]

You eat more vegetables

With my way of eating, you combine vegetables with all your meals and you step away from the (bad) habit of combining potatoes or pasta with everything. What's more, you will automatically substitute these fast carbohydrates (potatoes, bread, pasta, etc.) for vegetables, so that your vegetable consumption will increase.

Remember: vegetables are your key to a long life. Vegetables strengthen your immune system, detoxify your body and form the basis for a healthy lifestyle.

Or as Dr. Béliveau[3] states it in his book: "Vegetables are undeniably the foodstuffs which offer the most chance of avoiding all different kinds of cancer. People who eat lots of fruit and vegetables are twice less likely to have cancer."

You eat far fewer (unhealthy) fast carbohydrates

With my way of eating you always need to make a choice. You have to choose between proteins (fish, meat, cheese, etc.) with vegetables or carbohydrates (potatoes, pasta, etc.) with vegetables. In other words, you move away from the classic habit of eating potatoes, bread or pasta with every meal. If you still opt for carbohydrates, it is best to combine these with vegetables, so that your food intake has a higher fiber content, which in turn has a beneficial effect on blood sugar levels. What exactly is the problem with fast carbohydrates? Read more about it on page 182.

It gives you something stable to hold on to in a world of excess

In theory, you are still free to eat everything, but you now have a set of (combination) rules, to which you must adhere. This makes things clear and easy to manage, certainly in a world where there is an excess of choice. It brings calm and peace.

My way of eating has been inspired by the theory of a 'combination diet'. The founders of this theory were Dr. Shelton and Dr. Hay. Their versions of the combination diet are much stricter than mine. For this reason, I only retained their most important principles, so that my way of eating is feasible for everyday life in our modern world. People with serious stomach or intestinal issues will, however, benefit more from following a much more rigorous combination regime.

"Many people think that fattening sugars are mainly to be found in cookies, cakes, sweets and soft drinks, but in this way they overlook the most important source of daily sugars, a source that most people consume in large quantities two or three times a day; namely, bread, potatoes, pasta and rice."

KRIS VERBURGH[4]

[1] Annik Mollen (2012). *Kerngezond. Biofysisch evenwicht voor een optimaal celmilieu.* Leuven: LannooCampus.
[2] Dr. Fedon A. Lindburg (2009). *The G.I. Mediterranean Diet.* Berkeley, CA: Ulysses Press.
[3] Dr. Richard Béliveau is a leading expert in the field of cancer research and a professor of cancer prevention and treatment at the University of Quebec in Montreal.
[4] Dr. Kris Verburgh (2014). *The Food Hourglass - stay younger for longer and lose weight.* London: Harper Collins.

Pleasure, health, romance, a slim figure...
For me, they are all things that go together.
Only then can you have 'pure enjoyment'.

Fish is good for us:
It contains plenty of omega-3:

Photo: wild trout

"An insufficient consumption of fish, vegetables and fruit is estimated to cause ten times more cardio-vascular disease than the excess consumption of saturated fatty acids." [2]

Saturated fat

Strictly speaking, there is nothing wrong with saturated fat. It is much more important to limit your consumption of carbohydrates. The contribution of saturated fatty acids to cardio-vascular disease is (probably) only of importance in people whose consumption of carbohydrates is also high.[3]
In other words, if you eat lots of bread, potatoes, cakes, etc., you also need to watch your intake of saturated fats.

Why is saturated fat and carbohydrates not a good combination?
Carbohydrates can only be stored in the body in limited amounts: about 200 grams in your muscles and between 100 to 200 grams in your liver. When this capacity is used up, any remaining carbohydrates are converted into fat. If you keep on eating fat in this situation, you have a problem. Your body makes saturated fat and you continue to add more fat through your food intake, so that you have much more fat than you can possibly burn up. This excess body fat - primarily around your belly - causes an inflammatory reaction. Long-term inflammation can cause diseases such as insulin resistance, type-2 diabetes, cardio-vascular disease and other typically Western diseases, like cancer.[4] It is generally accepted that six out of every ten cases of cancer worldwide are caused by chronic inflammation.[5]

Bad fats are non-natural fats
Refined fats
I call them dead fats. 'Refined' means that they have been industrially processed at high temperatures and/or treated chemically in order to increase their yield and lengthen their storage life. As a result, most of their important nutritional elements are lost. Worse still, oils refined this way can also produce harmful side products, including trans fats. In addition, refined fats deprive your body of the vitamins, minerals and antioxidants you need, while giving little or nothing back in return.[6]

Trans fatty acids
Trans fatty acids are created by solidifying (hydrogenation) vegetable oils and are primarily found in industrially processed foods such as margarines, salty snacks, croissants, industrial-prepared meals, French fries, hamburgers, etc.

The most important message:
- don't be afraid of fats, but vary your intake of them;
- limit your intake of (fast) carbohydrates;
- eat lots of fish;
- limit your intake of omega-6 fats (sunflower oil, corn oil, soy oil, etc.);
- opt for natural products: if you see 'refined or hydrogenated fats' on the label, put it back on the shelf;
- eat more vegetables and fibers.

Fats in practice
Warm dishes
I mostly use extra virgin olive oil (mono-unsaturated fatty acids) to sauté or slow fry on a moderate heat. In addition, I also use coconut oil (saturated vegetable fat), because this oil works better at higher temperatures. Occasionally, I use good quality butter (saturated animal fat) for taste.

Never let your fat or oil burn!
If you can see and smell blue, smoky, pungent fumes, it is already too late. This will cause a chemical reaction that will not only ruin the flavor of your food, but will also damage your health. For this reason, I never allow my pan with oil or fat to stand on the cooker. I always add the food immediately. This lowers the temperature in the pan and helps to avoid any unpleasant surprises. The idea that foods like meat and mushrooms first need to be seared is not true. Meat still continues to lose its juices after it has been seared, and in the case of vegetables I actually want them to give off their juice, since this is the perfect basis for a really great sauce - as long as it isn't burned!

"Sear your meat so that it doesn't lose its juices is another of those stubborn myths." [7]

Cold dishes
In addition to extra virgin olive oil, I vary quite often with a selection of nut oils, such as walnut oil or hazelnut oil, which I use for cold dishes. It is best not to use nut oils for warm meals, since they burn faster at relatively low temperatures.

[1] Marcane F. Luxwolda (2012). *Omega-3 fatty acids and vitamin D in traditionally living East African populations. Lessons from evolution for a healthy life style.* Groningen: State University of Groningen.
[2][3][4] F.A.J. Muskiet, M.H.A. Muskiet & R.S. Kuipers. *Het failissement van de verzadigde vethypothese van cardiovasculaire ziektes.* Nederlands tijdschrift voor klinische chemie en laboratoriumgeneeskunde. 37:192-211.
[5] Richard Béliveau & Denis Gringas (2008). *Cuisiner avec les aiments contre le cancer.* Paris: Editions Robert Laffont.
[6] Fedon Alexander Lindberg (2006). *The Greek Doctor's Diet Cookbook.* London: Rodale International Ltd.
[7] Harold McGee (2004). *On food and cooking. The science and lore of the kitchen.* New York: Schribner.

Keep it practical

The recipes
The recipes in this book are written for two people unless otherwise stated. Olive oil, black pepper and sea salt are not included in the ingredients lists each time, but I assume that you already have these products in your home.

Don't get lost in the details
Cooking is all about balance. Nothing in life is black and white. There is no harm in eating French fries or a delicious dessert every once in a while. The problems start when you eat French fries every day - and the same applies to white bread, meat and sweetened fruit drinks. I follow my eating principles roughly 80% of the time. This is the cooking I like the most and the cooking I want to return to time after time. But if I am invited to a meal at a friend's house, I am the very last person to make comments about their food - even if they serve me French fries!

What does my daily menu look like? In the morning, I nearly always eat a fruit breakfast (see page 50). Since I never eat bread-based meals, I make no real distinction between lunch and dinner. All my recipes can either be eaten at midday or in the evening. At lunchtime, I usually opt for something quick and easy to make, which often means a salad. I prefer to eat warm in the evening. As snacks throughout the day, I nibble at nuts, dried fruit and dark chocolate (see page 49).

We are all pressed for time
Healthy eating doesn't happen all by itself. In life, you have to make choices: making a meal with vegetables takes more time than making a burger with a bun. But if you take the time, you get so much more in return. It makes the difference between falling asleep or bursting with energy. The most time-consuming element is shopping for the right ingredients; preparing the actual meals is less time-consuming. Try to organize yourself, so that you can do all your shopping in just two visits to the mall each week.

Fruit, herbs and spices are expensive?
Sadly, 'real' food is more expensive. If the government wants to do something about public health, it should make these ingredients less costly. It is often worth the effort to seek out a Moroccan shop: fruit, (fresh) herbs and spices are often much cheaper. You can usually buy a large sachet of turmeric for just 2 euros!

Work step by step
If you are used to classic Western food, my way of cooking and eating will probably require you to make a number of changes to the way you do things. Just take one step at a time, until you eventually make the new eating habits your own. You will quickly notice that you feel better. And before you know it, you won't ever want to eat any other way.

Live sensibly
Don't always allow yourself to be persuaded by what others say is good for you. Be aware and be critical. It is all about attitude, about the way you approach your life. In other words, it is about more than just food. It is also a question of exercise, respect for nature, making your own choices. For me, good health means being able to function at my maximum potential, so that I can enjoy life to the fullest. I am also curious about things and - I admit it! - a bit of a hedonist. I refuse to exclude any single ingredient from my diet and I never say 'you must not eat this'. But it is important to know what you can/should eat in large quantities and what you should eat more sparingly.

Salad with broccoli and avocado

WORK: 12 MINUTES - COOKING TIME: 7 MINUTES - SERVES 2

7 oz goat cheese
2 avocados
1 broccoli
1 handful of salad (mixed
    salad or lettuce)
sherry vinegar

Bring some water to the boil in a pan with a little salt, plenty of black pepper and a good splash of olive oil (see tip).
Cut off the broccoli florets and chop the stem into blocks (first removing the stem's hard outer skin). Boil the broccoli in the water for 5 minutes.
Cut the avocados in small cubes.
Pour off the water from the broccoli and return the pan briefly to the heat, so that any remaining water evaporates. Add a little olive oil and season with a little salt and pepper (be careful not to use too much, because the cooking fluid was already seasoned - taste it first!).
Remove the pan from the heat and add the avocado cubes. Next, add some sherry vinegar and about three-quarters of the goat cheese, which you can crumble in by hand. Stir briefly and carefully.
Place the salad on a plate and add the broccoli-avocado mix on top. Finish with the rest of the goat cheese.

Tip: boiling vegetables
I always add a little salt, plenty of black pepper and a good splash of olive oil to the water in which I boil my vegetables. This gives the vegetables much more flavor. You can do this with any vegetables you cook.

Tip: for a take-along lunch
If I make this recipe as a take-along lunch, I keep the salad separately with some extra nuts, which I can spread over this dish to give it a little extra 'bite'.

One of my favorite lunches: super-tasty.

Salad with ricotta and feta

WORK: 10 MINUTES - SERVES 2

VEGETABLES
4 tomatoes
1 red onion
1 red bell pepper

SALAD OR HERBS
flat-leaf parsley
2 spring onions

2 tablespoons of ricotta
1 slice of feta
juice of 1 lemon

Take a large bowl.
Cut the tomatoes and the red pepper into large pieces. Cut the red onions into fine, half rings. Finely chop the parsley and the spring onions. Place all the ingredients in the bowl.
Crumble the feta into the bowl and add the ricotta. Season well with plenty of black pepper and a little salt. Add a splash of olive oil and the lemon juice.
Stir all the ingredients well, so that all the flavors intermingle - because that is what makes this recipe so tasty!

Tip: for a take-along lunch
The flavor and structure of the vegetables improves the longer they are allowed to stand. This means that this recipe is ideal for a take-along lunch. You can add plenty of other herbs, depending on your personal preference (for example, basil).

Tasty, creamy and full of flavor.

Chickpeas with pan-fried bell peppers

WORK: 3 MINUTES - COOKING TIME: 7 MINUTES - SERVES 2

1 red bell pepper
1 yellow bell pepper
1 green bell pepper
1 red onion

1 can of pre-cooked chickpeas
1 teaspoon of cumin seeds

Put the cumin seeds in a pan for 2 to 3 minutes on a medium heat until the seeds' aroma is released. In the meantime, remove the seeds from the bell peppers and cut into strips. Cut the red onion into rings. Pour a good splash of olive oil into the pan and fry the vegetables until they are cooked. Season with salt and pepper. When the vegetables are ready, add the drained chickpeas. Allow them to cook with the peppers, until they are warmed through. Can be served either hot or cold.

Tip: flat-leaf parsley
Finely chopped flat-leaf parsley is a delicious addition to this recipe, especially if you are planning to use it for a take-along meal.

Delicious and filling
- both hot or cold.

Lacquered chicken with haricots verts

WORK: 5 MINUTES - COOKING TIME: 10 MINUTES - SERVES 2

2 chicken fillets
11 oz haricots verts
4 cloves of garlic

3 tablespoons of balsamic
    vinegar
3 tablespoons of (mild)
    soy sauce

Boil the haricots verts and the (whole) cloves of garlic until they are cooked through in a pan of water with a little salt, pepper and a splash of olive oil.
Cut the chicken into strips. Pour the soy sauce, balsamic vinegar and a tablespoon of olive oil into a pan. Fry the chicken in the pan until all the moisture is absorbed. Stir continually, especially at the last moment.
Serve the chicken with the haricots verts.
This dish is delicious either hot or cold.

Tip: garlic
Boiled garlic loses much of its powerful flavor, so that you can eat it whole. It melts like butter in your mouth and is surprisingly tasty, as well as being very healthy.

This chicken is so yummy!
And the garlic melts like
butter in your mouth.

The nicest compliment I ever had came from a 50-year-old woman, who in the meantime has lost 30 pounds thanks to my way of eating. She wrote to say that her husband had told her: 'I don't understand it. I see you eating all those nuts and using all that olive oil. In fact, I see you eating far more that you ever did before - and yet you still keep losing weight! No, I don't understand it. But whatever it is, just keep on doing it!" In other words: nuts don't make you fat!

You really don't have the time?

MIXED NUTS, DRIED FRUIT AND CHOCOLATE...
A DELICIOUS ENERGY BOOST OF VITAMINS AND MINERALS

At home, I always have a large glass jar filled with mixed nuts and dried fruit. Anyone who passes just puts in their hand and pulls out whatever they want. Ideal as a between-meals snack. On really busy days, I take a few handfuls of this mixture along in my lunchbox. It's a great midday meal that I can eat 'on the move'. Why not give it a try? You will soon find out just how scrumptious and filling it really is!

Non-spiced nuts
Walnuts, hazelnuts, almonds, pecan nuts, etc.
Nuts are packed with vitamins and minerals, such as magnesium. These are substances that most people are deficient in. Nuts are also an excellent source of beneficial 'good' fats. Walnuts, for example, contain omega-3 fatty acids. And to top it all, nuts are rich in fibers and valuable nutrients as well.

Dried fruit without added sugars
Dried sulfur-free apricots are ideal. Dried cranberries, goji berries and mulberries are all regarded as superfoods, because of their wide range of beneficial effects. Amongst other things, they stimulate the immune system, so that you are less likely to fall ill.
Dried dates, raisins and figs are less suitable, because they are too sweet.

Chocolate with 70% cocoa - and preferably more!
Dark (bitter-sweet) chocolate is rich in antioxidants and is a great source of energy. Cocoa contains the building blocks to make serotonin, which works as an anti-depressant in the body. That is why we feel so good after a delicious piece of bittersweet chocolate. But remember: milk chocolate does not have the same effect!

Fruit salad with coconut milk and mixed seeds

WORK: 15 MINUTES - SERVES 2

Mixed fruits of the season
coconut milk
mixed seeds (linseed, chia
  seeds, hemp seeds,
  pumpkin seeds, etc.)

Cut the fruit into pieces. Take about a quarter of the fruit and mix it in a blender, until it forms a coulis. Spoon the coulis, the coconut milk and the mixed seeds over the rest of the fruit.

Tip: coconut milk
Coconut milk is made from grated coconut mixed with water, from which the resulting liquid is then pressed out. As a result, coconut milk is very fluid. If you use more grated coconut, the fluid becomes thicker, so that we then speak of coconut cream. Be on your guard against coconut milk that contains industrial thickeners. Thickeners should never be used in coconut milk.

Tip: a fruit breakfast for winter
For a delicious winter breakfast you can add soaked and warmed prunes, cooked apples or pears, cinnamon and/or ginger powder. These delicious combinations will soon warm you up on a cold winter morning! And as far as your health is concerned, nothing beats a fruit breakfast. No other kind of breakfast can offer you so much in terms of vitamins, minerals and valuable nutrients.

Tip: seeds
Go to your local health food store, buy all different kinds of seeds and keep them together in the same jar. All you need to do each morning is open the lid, put in your hand and you have an instant portion of delicious mixed seeds. They give a real boost to your reserves of omega-3 fatty acids (present in linseed, hemp seeds and chai seeds) and are also rich in minerals.

I just can't miss my fruit breakfast.

This is what I eat every morning for breakfast. It is also great in smaller portions as a between-meals snack. Fruit salad is a huge bomb of essential fatty acids, vitamins, minerals and valuable nutrients.

This is most definitely one of my favorite
dishes. Deliciously smooth and full of

Omelet with boletus mushrooms

WORK: 10 MINUTES - COOKING TIME: 15 MINUTES - SERVES 2

4 eggs
1 shallot
30 cleaned boletus mush-
    rooms (or any other mush-
    room)
1 handful of curled parsley

Take a pan with a lid.
Beat the eggs and season with salt and pepper. Finely chop the shallot and parsley, and add then to the egg mixture.
Cut the mushrooms into half-centimeter slices and fry them on a medium heat in olive oil until both sides are golden brown, turning them carefully. Season with salt and pepper. When cooked, turn them out onto a plate. Return the pan to the heat, add the beaten egg mixture and pour in the mushrooms on top. Cover the pan with a lid. Do not stir, but allow the eggs to slowly congeal. You can sprinkle more parsley on top of the omelet, if you wish. The omelet is ready to serve when the upper surface is still slightly moist.

Tip: boletus mushrooms
I love wild mushrooms precisely because they are wild, free from all interference by man. Boletus are sometime referred to as the 'king' of wild mushrooms, since they are scarce and difficult to find. As a result, they are also expensive. Their peak growing season is in the fall. Of course, for this recipe you can always use ordinary mushrooms instead of wild ones.

Tip: cleaning mushrooms
It is best not to clean mushrooms with water, since in this way they absorb too much extra moisture. Instead, clean them with a soft brush and a knife. Cut off the hard part at the bottom of the stem and gently brush off any excess sand or soil.

A classic that is hard to beat.

Cauliflower and celery root with lentils, hazelnuts and hazelnut oil

WORK: 15 MINUTES - COOKING TIME: 30 MINUTES - SERVES 2

7 oz cauliflower
7 oz celery root
9 oz green lentils
1 handful of hazelnuts
1 bunch flat-leaf parsley

4 laurel leaves (optional)
1 teaspoon of cumin
   powder
hazelnut oil

Peel the celery root and cut it into large pieces. Cut off the cauliflower florets. Boil both vegetables for 4 minutes in some water with a little salt. Drain and keep to one side.
Preheat the oven to 350°F.
Arrange the vegetables in a baking dish. Season with the cumin powder and some black pepper. Pour over some olive oil and stir the ingredients thoroughly. Place the dish in the oven for 15 to 20 minutes.
In the meantime, rinse and boil the lentils with the laurel leaves for 20 to 30 minutes (or according to the instructions on the packet). Finely chop the parsley. Stir together all the ingredients: cauliflower, celery root, lentils, hazelnuts and parsley. Finish with a good splash of hazelnut oil.

Tip: a good recipe to make for more people
I like to make this dish when I have friends around for lunch. It is really tasty, whether served hot or cold, and is easy to make in large quantities.

Tip: nuts
For the hazelnuts in this recipe, I grill half of them and use the other half raw. You can also replace the hazelnuts and the hazelnut oil with walnuts and walnut oil.

Tip: lentils
See page 54.

A vegetable dish that I love... Unbelievably tasty!

Baked pears with goat cheese

WORK: 5 MINUTES · COOKING TIME: 10 MINUTES · SERVES 2

2 large blocks of goat
  cheese
3 pears

curly lettuce
2 stalks of fresh rosemary

1 handful of walnuts

FOR THE DRESSING:
3 tablespoons of honey
3 tablespoons of olive oil
1 tablespoon of balsamic
  vinegar
juice of ½ a lemon

Cut - but do not peel - the pears into four and remove the cores.
Fry the pears in a little olive oil on a light heat for about 10 minutes, until cooked through. Strip the leaves from the rosemary stalks and add them to the pan.
To make the dressing, stir together the honey, olive oil, balsamic vinegar and lemon juice in a bowl. Season with black pepper.
Wash the curly lettuce and arrange it on a plate. Place the pears in a star formation on top of the lettuce and put the goat cheese in the middle, covered with the honey dressing. Finish with the nuts, some black pepper and (optionally) a little extra olive oil.

Tip: goat cheese
If you use dry goat cheese, you can quickly fry the cubes on both sides, so that they get a delicious brown crust. This is not possible with fresh goat cheese.

The combination
of goat cheese and
pear is heavenly.

Ricotta-stuffed vegetables

WORK: 15 MINUTES · COOKING TIME: 30 MINUTES · FOR 6 STUFFED VEGETABLES

2 zucchini
2 tomatoes
2 sweet peppers (long or
   bell-shaped)
1 lb 2 oz ricotta
4 shallots
2 tablespoons of Parmesan
   cheese
2 tablespoons of fresh
   thyme leaves

Preheat the oven to 350°F.

Finely chop the shallots and mix them with the ricotta, thyme, Parmesan cheese and 4 tablespoons of olive oil. Season with plenty of pepper and a little salt. Cut the tops off the tomatoes and hollow them out. Cut the zucchini in two and scrape out the seed rib with a spoon. Cut the sweet peppers in half and remove the seeds. Fill all the vegetables with the ricotta mixture and place them in a baking dish. Bake for 30 minutes. Finish with some fresh thyme and olive oil.

Tip: ricotta

Ricotta is a delicious, creamy, white cheese with a grainy structure. Actually, it is not a cheese at all, rather a by-product of cheese. The whey that is left over from making other types of cheese is further reduced, resulting in what we now know as ricotta (the name actually means 're-cooked' or 'cooked twice'). The Italians discovered how to make it almost by accident. Ricotta is most frequently manufactured from sheep milk, but cow, goat and buffalo milk can also be used, which all have their own specific flavor. Ricotta is not a fatty cheese; quite the opposite, in fact.

The taste always has to be perfect, but if it looks good as well, then the pleasure is doubled.

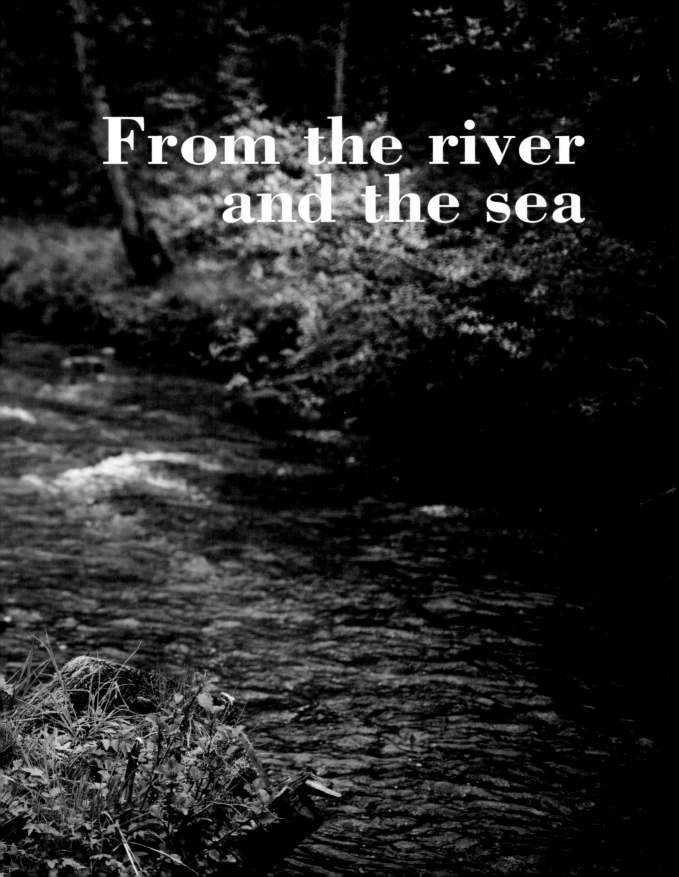

From the river and the sea

The story of the wild trout

For me, a holiday in the Ardennes without trout is unthinkable. The youthful memories it brings back are just too strong! What's more, wild trout contains omega-3. And eel and other river fish are also good for us, for the same reason.

By now, of course, we all know that the fish sold to us by the fishmonger and in supermarkets is farmed. But so too is the truite meunière that you can eat in the pleasant restaurants that line the banks of the babbling brooks and rapid rivers of the Ardennes. Trout farmed in special fish hatcheries are fattened with meal and other concentrates. This means that they cannot be compared with trout that have spent all their life fighting their way upstream, living from insects and small shrimp-like creatures that they catch along the way. Unfortunately, there are now very few wild trout swimming in our rivers.

The most commonly farmed trout species is the rainbow trout. Every rainbow trout that you get on your plate has been hatchery-raised and force-fed. Years ago, our waterways were packed with river trout, the salmo trutta fario. They are instantly recognizable from the magnificent red markings, dotted along the length of their powerful bodies. But now, even the fario is farmed on a large scale. So if you want to eat a real wild trout, you need to have a few days of patience - and a lot of persistence. A fishmonger in Malmedy - who admitted that he sold no wild fish in his shop - told us about a cafe owner, who knew someone who occasionally had some wild trout. After a long drive along the Amblève River, we finally found the man in question. He said that he would get back to us in a few days. It often happens nowadays that farmed fario are released back into the rivers. Anglers know when this is going to happen and the vast majority of these 'domesticated' fish are soon caught. Even so, there are always a few who manage to escape and breed. However, only expert fishermen know where these lucky few are likely to be found and when they can be fished.

A few days later, we did indeed get a telephone call from the man we had met. He had managed to catch a few of these wild trout and was keeping them for us in a tank. We cooked them on a grill on the banks of the river where the man had caught them. They were delicious. Farmed trout is often tasteless and the flesh is soft. But our wild fish had firm, white meat and a real trout taste - and there is no better taste in the world.

Grilled wild trout with mushrooms

WORK: 10 MINUTES · COOKING TIME: 15 TO 30 MINUTES · SERVES 2

2 trout
14 oz brown mushrooms
2 spring onions
4 stalks of rosemary
fresh or dried thyme

2 lemons

Prepare the vegetables and the fish beforehand at home.
Cut the mushrooms into four pieces and the spring onions into fine rings. Lightly fry the vegetables in a good splash of olive oil with a little salt, plenty of pepper and the thyme until everything is cooked through. Squeeze one of the lemons and add a little of the juice to the vegetables.
Clean the fish. Stuff the belly with rosemary. Season with salt and pepper and rub some olive oil into the skin of the fish. Now you are ready to leave!
Cook the fish and some slices of lemon on a grill. This should take between 15 and 30 minutes. Put a heat-resistant dish containing the vegetables on the grill as well, so that the contents can warm up gradually.

Nothing is more romantic than cooking fish in the open air, surrounded by Mother Nature.

Raw salmon with salmon eggs and tomatoes

WORK: 15 MINUTES - SERVES 4 (SEE TIP)

7 oz salmon fillets
1 pot of salmon eggs

2 tomatoes

chives
juice of ¼ lemon

Cut the tomatoes in quarters. Press each piece of the tomato flesh through a metal strainer, so that the skin and the seeds are kept in the strainer, producing a thick tomato pulp on the other side (see tip). Add to this tomato pulp two tablespoons of olive oil, a little lemon juice, some finely chopped chives and three-quarters of the salmon eggs. Season with salt and pepper.

Cut the salmon fillets into pieces and sprinkle them with a splash of olive oil and a little lemon juice. Season with salt and pepper. Divide the fish pieces between four glasses.

Add an equal amount of the tomato and salmon egg pulp to each of the four glasses. Finish with the remaining salmon eggs and chives.

Tip: portions
You can serve this dish as a snack or as a starter. Use 2 oz of salmon per person for a snack and 3 ½ oz for a starter. As a starter, I serve the salmon fillet in slices on a plate, covered with the tomato and salmon egg sauce. It is easy to make this sauce in advance, but only pour it over your salmon when your guests arrive. Otherwise, the moisture in the pulp will separate - which is not what you want.

Tip: thick tomato sauce
As an alternative, you can peel and de-seed your tomatoes and pulp the flesh in a blender. But I find it easier just to press it through a strainer.

A delicious combination...

Salmon fish balls with herbs and wasabi mayonnaise

WORK: 20 MINUTES - COOKING TIME: 15 MINUTES - FOR 6 TO 8 FISHBALLS

14 oz salmon fillets
2 spring onions
½ fresh, red chili pepper
2 cloves of garlic
1 bunch cilantro
juice of 1 lemon
3 tablespoons of sesame seeds
roasted sesame oil

FOR THE SAUCE:
mayonnaise
wasabi

Clean the salmon. Finely chop the fish, vegetables and herbs. Add a good splash of sesame seed oil and the lemon juice. Season with a little salt and plenty of pepper. Add the sesame seeds. Stir thoroughly and place in a blender (see tip). Mix to a firm fish paste (which still has a little bit of structure). Use the paste to make flattish fish balls and fry these for 10 to 15 minutes in the roasted sesame oil on a moderate heat. Mix together the mayonnaise and wasabi (vary the proportions according to your own preference).

Tip: red chili pepper
Don't be scared of using chili peppers. I used to think that chili was much too hot. But the fine red chili peppers of about 10 centimeters in length are not so spicy. However, they do give a little bit of extra bite to your recipes and are very healthy. Remove the seeds (these are the spiciest part) and remember not to rub your eyes!

Tip: blender
If you want to make a firm paste - of vegetables, fish or meat - it is important that you first finely chop all the ingredients and mix them together by hand before you put them in the blender. If you fail to do this, only the bottom part of the ingredients will be properly mixed by the blender. And the less fluid your pulp contains, the more difficult things will be. Mix in short bursts. If necessary, stir occasionally with a spoon. It is important that you do not over-mix, so that your mixture becomes flat and lifeless. You need to keep a bit of structure; otherwise the resulting paste becomes too dry when cooked.

Tip: wasabi and roasted sesame oil
Wasabi is Japanese mustard, but in this dish you can replace it with ordinary mustard, if you prefer. Nowadays, you can find wasabi and roasted sesame oil in any good supermarket.

Surprising and very tasty.

Spicy salmon with baked spinach

WORK: 15 MINUTES · COOKING TIME: 20 MINUTES · SERVES 2

2 pieces of salmon
1 lime

FOR THE SAUCE:
3 cloves of garlic
1 teaspoon of harissa

11 oz fresh spinach
1 teaspoon of nutmeg

Preheat the oven to 350°F.

Mix together (or grind with a mortar and pestle) the harissa, pepper, salt and some olive oil, until a thick paste is obtained. Rub this paste over and into the salmon and place the fish in a heat-resistant oven dish. Cut the lime in half and add it to the dish. Arrange the tomatoes around the fish. Bake for 20 minutes. Rinse the spinach, pat dry and cut into thin strips. The easiest way to do this is to roll up the spinach leaves. Place the spinach in a dish. Season with salt, pepper and nutmeg, and add a good splash of olive oil. Stir well, so that all the spinach is covered in oil. Add the spinach to the dish with the fish for the last 10 minutes of baking time.

Tip: spinach

I use a lot of spinach. It is not only very tasty, but is also packed with beta-carotene (fights cancer), vitamin K, folic acid and vegetable sterols. Even though spinach is also full of iron, it is not a good provider of this mineral to the body, since it also contains oxalic acid, which hinders the body's ability to absorb the iron.

The top layer of the spinach is crisp; the rest just melts in your mouth. A truly wonderful sensation...

Baked salmon with a thyme crust, tomatoes and green asparagus

WORK: 8 MINUTES - COOKING TIME: 20 TO 25 MINUTES - SERVES 2

14 oz salmon fillets
1 bunch of green
  asparagus
15 cherry tomatoes
1 handful of pine nuts
dried thyme
cumin seeds

Preheat the oven to 350°F.
Remove the bottom hard part of the asparagus. Place the asparagus in a baking dish. Pour over a splash of olive oil and season well with cumin seeds, black pepper and a little salt. Add the pine nuts. Stir thoroughly, so that all the asparagus are covered in oil.
Move the asparagus to one side of the dish. Place the tomatoes in the middle. Season with a little salt and pepper and a splash of olive oil. Cut the salmon fillets in pieces and splash them alongside the tomatoes. Generously season the fish with thyme, black pepper and a little salt. Drizzle with olive oil, so that the thyme is covered in it. Bake for 20 to 25 minutes.

Tip: spinach
For this recipe you can use spinach instead of asparagus. You can cook the spinach in the oven, as described above, or, alternatively, in a pan with a little nutmeg, salt and pepper (see page 88).

So little work, so much flavor!

Mahi-mahi fillet with ginger

WORK: 7 MINUTES · COOKING TIME: 15 MINUTES · SERVES 2

2 dorado fillets (skinned)
11 oz fresh young spinach

FOR THE SAUCE:
2 tablespoons of soy
    sauce
3 tablespoons of roasted
    sesame oil
2 tablespoons of lime juice
1 clove of garlic

1 spring onion

2 tablespoons of grated
    ginger

Preheat the oven to 350°F.
Clean the fish and place it in a heat-resistant dish, seasoned with some salt, pepper and olive oil. Put the dish in the oven for 15 minutes.
Fry the spinach briefly in a little olive oil, so that it remains half-raw. Season with salt and pepper.
Finely chop the garlic and the spring onion. Add the grated ginger and stir in the soy sauce, sesame oil and lime juice.
Place the spinach just off center on a plate. Remove the fish carefully from the oven dish with a large, flat spatula and place it alongside the spinach. Cover the fish with part of the sauce, and serve the remaining sauce separately in a sauceboat.

Tip: ginger
For further health and general information about ginger, please see page 134 (leek and carrot soup with ginger and chicken sate).

Mahi-mahi fillet
with a delicious
oriental sauce.

Baked mackerel with mustard and vine tomatoes

WORK: 10 MINUTES - COOKING TIME: 15 MINUTES - SERVES 2

4 mackerel fillets with
  skin
15 to 20 vine tomatoes
2 tablespoons of mustard
2 to 3 tablespoons of
  capers

SPICES FOR THE FISH:
½ red chili pepper
1 teaspoon of turmeric

Preheat the oven to 350°F.

Make shallow incisions in the fish, using a sharp knife (see photo). Make sure you do not cut all the way through!

Chop the half chili pepper into fine rings and mix with the turmeric, salt, pepper and 2 tablespoons of olive oil. Rub or brush this spicy mix all over the fish fillets. Place the fillets in a baking dish, with the skin side on top. Arrange the drained capers around the fish.

Mix the mustard with a tablespoon of olive oil. Smear this mixture over the vine tomatoes (this is most easily done with your fingers). Place the tomatoes alongside the fish.

Bake for 15 minutes.

Tip: turmeric
I have used a small amount of turmeric in this dish, more for the color than for the flavor. This is why this recipe is not included in the 'turmeric' section of the book.

Scrumptious mackerel with spicy tomatoes.

Cod with mustard-soy sauce and tomatoes

WORK: 6 MINUTES · COOKING TIME: 15 TO 20 MINUTES · SERVES 2

2 cod fillets

4 tomatoes

3 tablespoons of mustard
3 tablespoons of soy sauce

Preheat the oven to 350°F.

Finely slice the tomatoes. Remove all the hard, white parts. Make two piles of tomato slices in a baking dish, with one slice half on top of another, like tiles on a roof. Season with black pepper.

Mix the mustard and soy sauce with 2 tablespoons of olive oil. Pour a few spoonfuls of the resulting sauce over the tomatoes.

Place the cod fillets on top of the tomatoes and spoon over the remaining mustard-soy sauce. Bake for 15 to 20 minutes.

Tip: portions

Sometimes I make two piles of tomatoes and fish per person, depending on the thickness of the cod fillets and how hungry my guests are. If you use a loin fillet of cod - which is usually thicker - one portion of tomatoes and fish per person is generally enough.

This is my best and simplest recipe ever!

Whoever loves the sea
will love this recipe.

Romance doesn't happen by
itself; you need to create it.

It is about inspiration.
It is about creativity.
It is about surprise.

If you need to talk about romance, it loses its magic.
The power of romance lies in its mysticism.
It is about giving a new dimension - your dimension - to love.
Losing yourself in the moment, in the setting, in each other.
Experiencing your dreams as reality.
Allowing your soul to be touched by the beauty of this unique
instant in time.

Shellfish and crustaceans

Minute-fried scallops

WORK: 10 MINUTES - COOKING TIME: 1 MINUTE - SERVES 2

4 fresh scallops
5 black olives (without stones)
1 tablespoon of capers
1 lemon

Preheat the oven to 350°F.
Finely chop the olives and capers. Peel the lemon (leaving the hard, white part). Slice the peel into thin strips. Stir thoroughly and season with salt, pepper and a little olive oil.
Finely slice the scallops and arrange them in a circle on a heat-resistant plate, one on top of the other (in a roof-tile pattern). Place a spoonful of the olive mixture in the middle of the scallop circle.
Bake for 1 minute. Finish with some olive oil, black pepper and a little salt.

Beautifully flavored scallops that melt in your mouth.

Venus clams in a soy sauce, ginger and garlic soup

WASHING: 10 MINUTES - WORK: 5 MINUTES - COOKING TIME: 5 MINUTES - SERVES 2

1 lb 5 oz Venus clams (see tip)
3 cloves of garlic
0.5 inch of fresh ginger
soy sauce (not sweet, but mild)
juice of ½ lime

Wash the Venus clams thoroughly (see tip).
Pour one-third of the soy sauce into a pan with two-thirds of water (enough to nearly cover the Venus clams when they are added later). Place the pan on a medium heat. Finely slice the garlic and add to the pan. Finely chop the ginger (peeling is not necessary) and also add to the pan. Next, add the lime juice. Season well with black pepper. Do not add any extra salt: the soy sauce is salty enough.
When the soy soup begins to boil, add the Venus clams. Cook for about five minutes, or until all the clams have opened.
Serve immediately. The delicious soup can also be served as a beverage.

Tip: Venus clams
I love Venus clams, even if only for their name! But if you can't find any clams, cockles will do instead.

Tip: washing Venus clams
Venus clams live buried in the sand. For this reason it is important to wash them thoroughly before cooking. This takes time, but it is worth it: you don't want a mouthful of sand in your soy soup! Place the clams in cold water until they open. Rinse them and change the water. Do this two or three times.

Tip: with fresh spring onions
Finely chop two spring onions and add them to the pan for the last half minute of the cooking time.

Sensual, scrumptious and heart-warming.

Fried celery root and endives with shrimps and hazelnuts

WORK: 6 MINUTES - COOKING TIME: 12 MINUTES - SERVES 2

11 oz celery root
3 endives
5 oz grey shrimps
1 handful of grilled hazel-
    nuts
hazelnut oil

Peel the celery root, cut into 1-centimeter cubes and fry in a pan with a little olive oil until cooked through. Stir regularly, so that the cubes do not burn.

In the meantime, cut the endives into thin strips. When the celery root is cooked, add the endives to the pan. Continue cooking, until the endive strips begin to shrink. Season with salt and pepper. Divide the vegetables between the plates. Sprinkle the shrimps and the walnuts on top. Finish with a drizzle of hazelnut oil.

Unbelievably tasty; I love the structure and the flavor combinations.

Cauliflower puree with shrimps and truffle

WORK: 5 MINUTES - COOKING TIME: 10 MINUTES - SERVES 2

½ cauliflower
4 oz peeled shrimps
truffle oil (or olive oil)
truffle (optional)

Cut the cauliflower into pieces, including the stem (having first removed the hard skin). Boil in lightly salted water until cooked through. Pour off the water and return the pan to the heat. Add a good splash of olive oil and fry the cauliflower for a further few minutes. Puree the cauliflower using a potato masher (see tip). Season with plenty of black pepper and a little fleur de sel. Remove the pan from the heat and stir in three-quarters of the shrimps. Spoon the cauliflower puree onto the plates. Sprinkle the rest of the shrimps on top. Finish with a dash of truffle oil and (optionally) a few slices of truffle.

Tip: use a potato masher, not a food processor
Do not use a food processor for mashing. This results in a formless, homogenous mass. Instead, use a potato masher, which will allow you to retain some structure in your puree. This is not only healthier, but also more pleasant to eat. It at least gives you something to bite on!

Tip: portions
If I make this dish as a starter, I use 2 ½ oz of shrimps per person. If I make it as a main course - and I often cook it for lunch - I use about 3 ½ oz of shrimps per person. For lunch, I only use olive oil. Even without the truffle and the truffle oil, this recipe is super-tasty.

Pour on a little bit of truffle oil and you immediately have an exquisite dish.

A delicious and festive meal.

Bouillabaisse with shellfish

WORK: 10 MINUTES - COOKING TIME: 25 MINUTES - SERVES 2

1 fennel

1 leek (with leaves)
2 tomatoes
1 small can of tomato
  paste (70 g)
4 cloves of garlic

6 scampi (with their
  heads)
10 mussels
10 Venus clams
11 oz sea devil
7 oz mullet

Cut the leek and fennel into large pieces. Cut the garlic cloves in half. Lightly fry the vegetables in a pan with a good splash of olive oil. Cut the tomatoes into large pieces (first removing the hard, white parts) and add them to the pan. Cook this vegetable mixture for a few minutes. Add the tomato paste and enough water to barely cover the vegetables. When the vegetables are cooked through, add the fish (cut into pieces) and the shellfish. Simmer the bouillabaisse until everything is fully cooked.

Tip: what fish and what shellfish?
The answer to this question is simple: whichever fish and shellfish you most enjoy. You can also make your choice to reflect availability during the different seasons. However, it is important to choose firm fish that will not fall apart during the cooking. Sea devil, mullet, brill and loin of cod are all excellent.

Tip: if you have guests
You can make the soup without the fish earlier in the day. Cook the vegetables until they are al dente and then keep the pot aside for later. When your guests arrive, heat up the vegetable soup. When it boils, add the fish and the shellfish. Serve in an attractive bowl.

Lentil soup with turmeric

WORK: 15 MINUTES - COOKING TIME: 20 MINUTES - SERVES 2

9 oz orange lentils
2 onions
3 cloves of garlic
1.5 inches of fresh ginger
1 large tablespoon of
    turmeric
coconut milk (optional)

Rinse the lentils in cold water. Place them in a pot and add five times as much fresh water. Bring to the boil and simmer for 15 to 20 minutes (or in accordance with the instructions on the packet). In the meantime, finely chop the onion and garlic.
Using a different pot, heat a good splash of olive oil on a moderate heat. Don't allow the oil to get too hot! Add the turmeric and plenty of black pepper. Stir thoroughly. Add the onion and garlic, and fry gently until nicely glazed. If the pot becomes too dry, add a little more olive oil or a splash of water. Season with salt.
Add the turmeric mixture to the lentils. Grate in the ginger. Allow everything to cook for a little while longer and then mix finely with a hand mixer. Finish with a spiral of coconut milk (optional).

Tip: orange lentils
So delicious, yet so simple. There are several different kinds of lentils, but the main advantage of the orange variety is that they only take 15 to 20 minutes to cook. They cook down to a mushy pulp, but don't worry: this makes them ideal for a soup. Well worth a try!

Tip: health
This is a soup that actually makes you healthier. You might even call it an anti-cancer soup. I know that you need to be careful with claims of this kind, but all the ingredients in the soup - turmeric, garlic, ginger, onion and lentils - have been shown by reputable scientific studies to be both super-healthy and cancer fighting.

A soup that makes you healthier.

Skate with capers, spinach and tomato

WORK: 10 MINUTES · COOKING TIME: 20 MINUTES · SERVES 2

2 pieces of skate wing
3 tomatoes
11 oz spinach
1 lemon
6 tablespoons of drained
    capers
1 teaspoon of turmeric

Make a sauce using the turmeric, a little salt, plenty of black pepper and a good splash of olive oil. Rub the sauce into the skate wings and place them in a heat-resistant oven dish.

Preheat the oven to 350°F.

Cut the tomatoes in four, remove the insides and collect the fluid.

Cut the flesh of the tomato quarters into crescents. Add some olive oil and the tomato fluid. Season with salt and pepper. Pour this tomato mix into the oven dish. Scatter the capers around the fish and the tomatoes. Place the halved lemon in the dish as well.

Put the dish into the oven for 20 minutes.

In the meantime, lightly fry the spinach in a pan with a little olive oil, salt and pepper.

Arrange everything neatly on the plates and sprinkle more capers on top of the fish.

Not much work, but truly delicious
with those crunchy capers.

Skate with thick tomato sauce and capers

WORK: 15 MINUTES - COOKING TIME: 15 TO 20 MINUTES - SERVES 2

2 skate wings
20 mini-tomatoes
4 tablespoons capers

1 teaspoon turmeric
1 lime

Preheat the oven to 350°F.

Rub the skate wings with olive oil and season them with salt and pepper. Place the wings in a casserole dish. Bake for about 20 minutes.

Cut the tomatoes in half and fry them in a little olive oil. After 5 minutes add the turmeric and plenty of black pepper. Continue cooking until the tomatoes have reduced considerably in size. Season with a little salt. Finally, add the capers.

Cut the lime into two equal halves. Place them in a non-stick pan without fat on a moderate heat, with the cut faces against the pan bottom. Remove the limes when they begin to caramelize.

Arrange everything neatly on the plates.

This is one of my husband's very favorite dishes.

Carrot and leek soup with ginger and chicken sate

WORK: 20 MINUTES - COOKING TIME: 15 MINUTES - SERVES 2

2 chicken fillets
4 large carrots
½ leek (white part only)
1.5 inches of ginger root, grated
1 teaspoon of turmeric
roasted sesame seeds
soy sauce
balsamic vinegar

Clean the carrots and leek, and cut them into rings. Lightly fry them in a good splash of olive oil until nicely glazed. Add the ginger, turmeric, plenty of black pepper and a little salt. Stir thoroughly. Add enough water to just cover the vegetables and simmer for 10 to 15 minutes, or until the vegetables are cooked through.

Cut the chicken fillets into pieces and thread them onto two wooden skewers. Pour 4 tablespoons of olive oil, 4 tablespoons of soy sauce and 4 tablespoons of balsamic vinegar in a pan. Cook the chicken skewers in this mixture until the meat is cooked through. Season with black pepper (no salt). Remove the skewers from the pan and cover them with sesame seeds.

Mix the vegetables with a mixer until they form a thick soup.

Spoon some of this soup into a shallow plate and place the sates to one side (see photo). Serve the rest of the soup in a separate bowl. Finish with some extra sesame seeds.

Tip: ginger

Ginger can really bring a recipe to life. For this reason, it is a must-have in my kitchen. It stimulates your appetite, improves your blood circulation and has a deliciously warming aroma. Usually, I do not remove the peel, since most of the important nutritional elements are either in or just under this peel. The best way to use ginger in your cooking is therefore to grate it. For centuries, ginger has not only been found in the cook's larder, but also in the doctor's medicine chest. Modern research has shown that ginger relieves inflammation and has a positive effect on certain cancers.

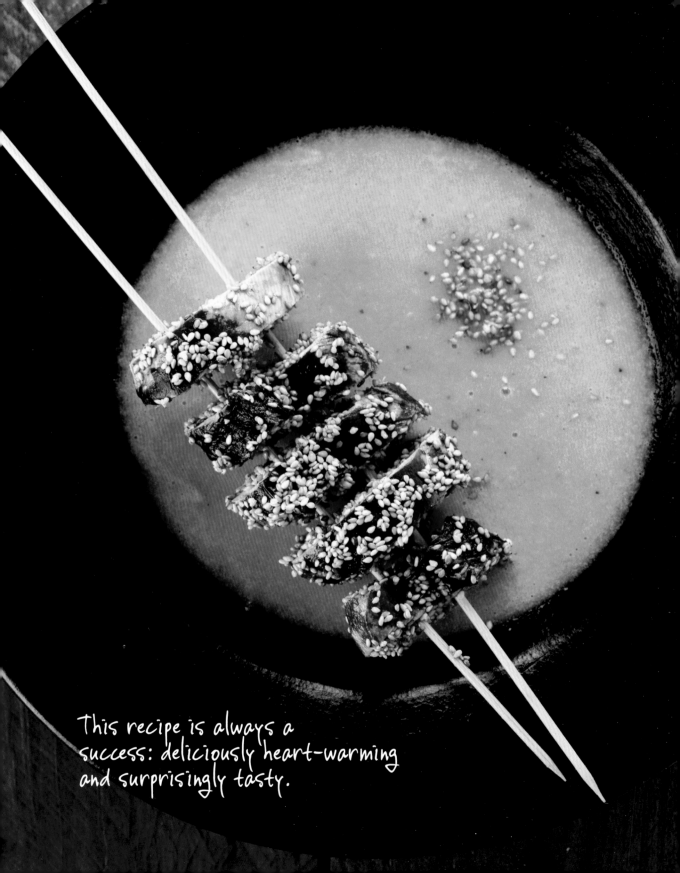

This recipe is always a
success: deliciously heart-warming
and surprisingly tasty.

Spicy curry soup with chicken and vegetables

WORK: 10 MINUTES - COOKING TIME: 30 MINUTES - SERVES 2

14 oz chicken fillets
2 stalks green celery
2 carrots
1 leek
4 shiitake or 8 brown
   mushrooms
4 cloves of garlic

1 level tablespoon of
   turmeric
curry paste

Wash the celery, carrots and leek and cut them into rings. Slice the garlic and cut the chicken into strips.
Put a large pot on the stove with a good splash of olive oil. Add all the vegetables and the garlic. Stir-fry for about 5 minutes.
Mix 3 tablespoons of red curry paste with a little water and add to the vegetables. Add the chicken strips and the turmeric. Season well with plenty of black pepper. Add enough water to barely cover all the ingredients. Cover with a lid and simmer for 20 to 30 minutes.
Cut the mushrooms into slices and add them to the pot for the last 5 minutes of cooking time.
Serve the soup in shallow bowls.

Tip: red curry paste
There are many different types of curry. The important thing is to use curry paste, and not powder. This particular dish should be spicy, so you can choose a 'hot' variety. In general, Western curry products are milder than their Asian equivalents. So begin by adding 2 tablespoons and then have a quick taste. If the dish is not yet hot enough, add another tablespoon and taste again. Carry on like this until you have the strength you want.

Tip: shiitake mushrooms
This is one of the most nutritional of all mushrooms. They are extremely rich in beneficial substances that strengthen our immune system. Always make sure that shiitakes are cooked through. Raw shiitakes can sometime cause serious allergic reactions.

Whenever I come home feeling cold and tired, I always serve this heartwarming and invigorating soup. It's a meal in itself!

Chicken with turmeric and pomegranate

WORK: 15 TO 20 MINUTES - COOKING TIME: 30 MINUTES - SERVES 2

2 chicken legs

2 red onions
1 pomegranate
1 tablespoon turmeric
3 laurel leaves
2 cinnamon sticks

Cut the chicken legs into two pieces across the joint. Place the two pieces next to each other in a pot and add enough water to barely cover them. Add the turmeric, a splash of olive oil, plenty of black pepper, a little salt, the laurel leaves and the cinnamon sticks. Bring to the boil and cook for 20 to 30 minutes (depending on the size of the chicken pieces). Preheat the oven to 350°F. Cut the onion into thin slices. Place them in a baking dish and sprinkle with a few spoonfuls of olive oil. Cover with a lid or aluminum foil. Bake for 20 minutes. In the meantime, remove the seeds from the pomegranate (see tip) and cut it into pieces. Bring all the ingredients together in a single pot and allow them to simmer for a further 5 minutes. Serve in shallow bowls.

Tip: how do I get the seeds out of a pomegranate?
See page 141.

Tip: pomegranates and health
Numerous research studies have shown that pomegranates are really good for your health. Their extremely high levels of antioxidants help us to fight the free radicals in our body that can cause both the premature ageing of cells and a number of serious diseases, including several types of cancer (such as prostate, intestinal and breast cancers). The properties of the antioxidants in pomegranates also give us added protection against cardiovascular disease and likewise have a beneficial neurological effect. When they are in season, I also use pomegranates in my fruit breakfast (see page 50).

Tip: pomegranates and meat
Iran has become the center of modern pomegranate production. They literally have pomegranate forests. For us, it is perhaps a slightly strange idea to serve meat with pomegranates, but this is common practice in Iran.

Warm and tasty
oriental flavors.

Zucchini with raw ham

WORK: 15 MINUTES · COOKING TIME: 15 MINUTES · SERVES 2

2 zucchini
16 slices of raw ham
    (prosciuto crudo, Ganda
    ham)
1 lemon
dried thyme

Preheat the oven to 350°F.
Cut the zucchini into quarters lengthwise. Cut out the seed rib.
Place the zucchini quarters in a dish. Add a good splash of olive oil
and season well with plenty of dried thyme, lots of pepper and a
little salt. Make sure you don't use too much salt, because the ham
is already salty. Rub the oil and the seasoning over the zucchini,
until they are all coated.
Wrap each piece of zucchini in two slices of ham.
Put the zucchini on the grill in the oven for 10 to 15 minutes.
For the last 5 to 7 minutes of cooking time add the halved lemon
(cut sides against the metal), until it begins to color.

Tip: main course
Add a few whole tomatoes to the grill and let them cook alongside the
zucchini. Serve this with a piece of meat: rack of lamb or fried steak.
Season the tomatoes with a little olive oil and some pepper and salt.
This adds lots of extra flavor.

Good to look at, good to eat,
simple to make.

Spicy ground lamb on skewers with curried tomato sauce

WORK: 15 MINUTES - COOKING TIME: 15 MINUTES - FOR 4 TO 6 SKEWERS

14 oz ground lamb (see tip)
4 spring onions
6 pieces of dried tomato in olive oil
2 cloves of garlic
1 bunch cilantro

FOR THE 3-MINUTE SAUCE:
2 large tomatoes
2 tablespoons of tomato paste
2 tablespoons of mild, red curry paste

sweet paprika powder

Preheat the oven to 350°F.
Finely chop the spring onions, dried tomato, garlic and the cilantro. Mix these ingredients with the ground lamb and season with salt and pepper. Press the mince around the wooden skewers and place them on the grill in the oven for 10 to 15 minutes.
Quarter the tomatoes and remove the insides (seeds, fluid and any hard, white parts). Put the tomato pieces in the blender with the tomato paste, the red curry paste and 2 tablespoons of olive oil. Mix thoroughly into a thick sauce. Don't overmix - make sure that your sauce still retains some structure (see tip). Serve the skewers with the sauce, sprinkled with a little sweet paprika powder.

Tip: ground lamb
Ground lamb is usually sold as a combination of two-thirds lamb's mince and one-third pork mince, since this makes it easier to work with. 100% ground lamb is fairly dry and crumbles more easily. But both kinds can be used and both are very tasty.

Tip: red curry paste
There are many different kinds of curry paste on the market. They range from mild to super-strong. They can all be used, depending on your personal preference. I like to use a milder paste and I taste my dish regularly during preparation, to avoid any unpleasant - and hot - surprises.

Tip: 3-minute sauce
This is a delicious sauce. Because it contains fresh tomatoes, some of the juice may rise to the surface if the sauce is left to stand for a time. This is not a problem. Just pour off the excess fluid and give the sauce a good stir.

Practical, pretty
and oh so good!

Spicy salad with steak and pomegranate

WORK: 15 MINUTES · COOKING TIME: 6 MINUTES · SERVES 2

14 oz steak
1 pomegranate (see tip)
1 red bell pepper
1 radicchio lettuce (or
    some other type of
    lettuce)

FOR THE SAUCE:
4 to 6 tablespoons of
    roasted sesame oil
juice of 3 limes
½ red chili pepper
1 bunch cilantro
red currants (optional)
fleur de sel

Fry the steak in a little olive oil for about 3 minutes on each side until it is nice and pink. Allow the meat to rest under a piece of aluminum foil.

In the meantime, make the salad. Remove the seeds from the pomegranate. Cut the red bell pepper into fine slices. Add the pomegranate seeds. Place these ingredients on top of the radicchio lettuce in a bowl.

For the sauce, remove the seeds and the white parts from the red chili pepper and cut it into thin, half-rings. Finely chop the cilantro. Mix these together with the sesame oil, lime juice, red currants, some black pepper and fleur de sel. Stir thoroughly. Cut the meat into slices. Pour part of the sauce over the vegetables and part over the meat.

Tip: how do you get the seeds out of a pomegranate?
See page 141.

Tip: this dish as an appetizer
I often serve this dish (but without the salad) as an appetizer. I cut the meat into smaller pieces and serve them with the sauce.

The flavors are
so intense! Spicy
and sensual.

Magret de canard with cranberries and pomegranate

WORK: 20 MINUTES - COOKING TIME: 20 MINUTES - SERVES 2

1 large duck breast
  (with fat)
1 pomegranate
7 oz fresh cranberries
1 piece of chocolate
  (at least 70% cocoa)
1 glass of red wine
3 tablespoons of sugar
  (see tip)

Remove the seeds from the pomegranate (see tip on page 141).
Preheat the oven to 350°F. Do not remove the skin from the duck breast, but make diagonal incisions on the surface of the fat, so that the heat of the pan can penetrate the meat. Fry the breast on the fat side (without adding additional fat) for 4 minutes. Turn the meat over and cook the other side for a further 3 minutes. Remove the pan from the heat and place in the oven for 7 minutes.
Cook the cranberries with the sugar in a little water. When all the berries have opened, add the pomegranate seeds and simmer gently for a further 5 minutes. Remove the duck from the oven, wrap it in aluminum foil and put it aside. Pour the fat out of the pan, but keep the scraps of meat from the cooking and return to a low heat. Add the red wine. When the wine is warm, add the chocolate and let it melt. Season with plenty of black pepper. Allow the sauce to thicken.
Slice the duck breast and serve it with a portion of the cranberry mix. Pour the sauce over the meat or serve separately in a sauceboat.

Tip: sugar
Try using coconut sugar instead of ordinary sugar (see the tip on coconut sugar on page 174).

Tip: fresh cranberries
Europeans first learned about these berries from the Indians. Because the tops of the shrubs looked like the neck and head of a crane (the bird) when blowing in the wind during the flowering season, European colonists decided to call this species the crane berry, which was later shortened to cranberry. Cranberries are one of the healthiest of all berries. They are packed with antioxidants and flavonoids, which help strengthen our immune system. Fresh cranberries are available from October to January.

For when you want something a little more festive...

Grilled quail with apple

WORK: 10 MINUTES - COOKING TIME: 20 MINUTES - SERVES 2

4 quails
2 apples

1 tablespoon of cinnamon
  powder
1 tablespoon of curry
  powder

Preheat the oven to 350°F. Cut the quails in two. Mix the curry powder with 2 tablespoons of olive oil and rub this mixture into the flesh of the birds.
Cut the apples into slices with a thickness of 0.5 centimeter (there is no need to remove the core). Mix the cinnamon powder with 2 tablespoons of olive oil and brush or rub this mixture over the apple slices.
Broil the quails and apples for 10 to 15 minutes, until everything is properly cooked.

Tip: outdoor grill
You can easily prepare this dish on the grill. However, be careful not to burn it! Burned food is very unhealthy. That is why I prefer to work with a gas BBQ with a lid. This gives you an oven effect, whilst at the same time making it easier to alter the temperature, allowing you more control over the cooking process. It also gives you more freedom as a hostess to enjoy the company of your guests, since you don't need to be standing constantly over the hot coals.

Everyone loves
this recipe.

Quail with pan-fried carrots and a hazelnut sauce

WORK: 20 MINUTES · COOKING TIME: 40 TO 60 MINUTES · SERVES 2

4 quails
4 large carrots
juice of 1 orange
1 handful of roasted
   hazelnuts
a little good butter

FOR THE STUFFING:
2 brown mushrooms
1 onion
dried thyme
a splash of cognac

Finely chop the mushrooms and onion. Mix them together with 2 tablespoons of olive oil, some thyme and a splash of cognac. Season with salt and pepper. Use this mixture to stuff the quails. Preheat the oven to 350°F.

Fry the quails on all sides in a good splash of olive oil. Put the pan in the oven and allow the birds to cook for a further 20 minutes.

Wash the carrots (unless they are dirty, there is no need to peel them). Boil them until they are cooked through. Pour off the water and sauté the carrots in a little olive oil. Crush the hazelnuts into rough pieces, using a mortar and pestle. Roast them briefly in a little butter and add the orange juice.

Serve the carrots with the hazelnut sauce and arrange the quails alongside.

Tip: quails

Quails are small birds from the pheasant family. They have deliciously tasty meat. Young quails can be cooked 'rosé', so that they only need an extra 10 minutes in the oven. These young birds have white skin and pink meat. The older a quail is, the greyer the color of its meat and the yellower the color of its skin become.

Refined flavors, yet simplicity itself to make.

Rack of lamb with red beet in a curry sauce

WORK: 10 MINUTES - COOKING TIME: 30 MINUTES - SERVES 2

1 rack of lamb
2 red beets (see tip)
3 tablespoons of red
curry paste (see tip)
coconut milk (see tip)

Wash the beets thoroughly and cut into thin sticks. Put the sticks in a shallow pot and add coconut milk until the beet is two-thirds covered. Add the red curry paste (in an amount that reflects your personal preference). Stir carefully. Simmer for 25 to 30 minutes, until the beets are cooked through. Check regularly to ensure that the mixture does not dry out. If necessary, add a little water. Preheat the oven to 350°F. Cut the fat off the rack of lamb and fry it in a pan with a little olive oil for 2 to 3 minutes on each side. Season with salt and pepper. Put the pan in the oven and cook for a further 8 to 10 minutes. Remove the lamb from the oven and let it rest under a sheet of aluminum foil, so that the heat can penetrate the meat and the juices can settle. Cut the rack into individual cutlets and serve with the curried beet.

A dish that makes you happy. The red beet is so yummy!

Tip: red beet
Making red beet in this way is super-tasty. You have really got to try it, even if you are not a big fan of beet. I guarantee that you will be pleasantly surprised!

Tip: red curry paste
Use curry paste, and not curry powder. The beet certainly needs to taste hot and spicy, but everyone has his or her own personal 'heat limit' as far as curry is concerned. For this recipe I use a 'mild to hot' paste. There are so many different curries on the market that it is always difficult to know how much to use. Don't be too hasty. Begin with 2 tablespoons and taste the result. If you need to add more, you can - right up to the very last moment before serving.

Tip: coconut milk
Coconut milk is made from grated coconut mixed with water, from which the resulting liquid is then pressed out. As a result, coconut milk is very fluid, as fluid as ordinary milk. Do not use coconut cream; this is much thicker. The cream is ideal for breakfast, but not for cooking. If you can only find coconut cream at your local store, you can dilute it with water. Always choose 100% coconut milk without additives and thickeners.

Eggplant stuffed with ground lamb

WORK: 10 MINUTES · COOKING TIME: 45 MINUTES · SERVES 2

1 eggplant
11 oz ground lamb
1 onion
1 can of concentrated
  tomato paste (70 g)
2 cloves of garlic
1 teaspoon of cumin seeds
  (optional)

Preheat the oven to 350°F.

Halve the eggplant lengthwise. Slightly hollow out both halves with a knife. The flesh you remove can be added to the filling later.

Make incisions in the flesh of the two halves, but make sure you don't cut through the outer skin. Brush the incised flesh with olive oil and season with salt and pepper. Bake for 30 minutes.

Finely chop the garlic and the onion. Briefly roast the cumin seeds in a dry pan, until the aroma is released. Add a good splash of olive oil, followed by the garlic and the onion. When the vegetables are nicely glazed, add the ground lamb. Stir continually, so that the meat loosens and does not stick together.

Finally, add the tomato paste and stir well.

Fill the eggplant halves with this mixture and return them to the hot oven for a further 10 to 15 minutes.

This is one of my all-time favorite dishes. The flavors are so intense.

Oven-cooked fillet of beef with a cauliflower and tomato couscous

WORK: 10 MINUTES - COOKING TIME: 45 MINUTES - SERVES 2

2 beef fillets
1 cauliflower
6 medium-sized toma-
   toes

3 cloves of garlic
1 bunch flat-leaf parsley

Cut off the outer half centimeter from the cauliflower. Rub these pieces between your fingers, until they crumble into a 'couscous'. Use the rest of the cauliflower for another recipe (perhaps a cauliflower puree) or cut it into pieces for use as an appetizer with your aperitif.

Place the cauliflower couscous in a pan with the garlic cloves (peeled and whole). Add enough water to just cover the ingredients. Boil for 5 minutes until the cauliflower is al dente. Pour away the water and put the pan with the cauliflower back on the heat. Add a good splash of olive oil and lightly sauté the couscous for a further 5 minutes. When the couscous is cooked through, carefully stir in the finely chopped flat-leaf parsley. Season with salt and pepper.

Preheat the oven to 350°F.

Brown the beef fillets on both sides in a pan with a little olive oil. Add the tomatoes and put the pan in the oven for 4 to 7 minutes. Remove the beef and wrap it in aluminum foil, so that the heat can penetrate the meat and the juices can settle. Allow the tomatoes to cook further in the oven.

Arrange everything neatly on the plates: first the cauliflower couscous, with the tomatoes on top and the sliced fillets of beef alongside.

Admit it: cauliflower couscous sounds interesting — and it tastes divine.

Enjoying the occasional 'sin' is an art

Eating dessert every now and again can do no harm. On the contrary, they are 'food for the soul'. The main problem is that for people with high insulin levels (in other words, people who eat large quantities of fast carbohydrates and sweet foods every day) these desserts can also cause inflammation that can lead to illness and disease. For this reason, we also need to consider white bread, pasta and French fries as 'desserts'.

I have never tried to find a 'healthy' dessert: that is simply fooling yourself. Desserts, by definition, are unhealthy. Even eating fruit after a meal is a bad choice. The fruit ends up in a warm stomach, in which the other food you have just eaten has not yet been properly digested. And as everyone knows: when fruit is subjected to warmth, it begins to ferment. The result is a swollen stomach and digestive problems.

If I eat dessert, I go for the real thing. I am not interested in 'light' products. If I am going to 'sin', then I want to sin properly. At least in this way I am satisfied, both physically and psychologically. My craving falls away - until the next time, at least. And you don't need to eat really large portions to have the desired effect. Quite the opposite.

Take a chocolate dessert, for example. That is food for both body and soul! Something I can really enjoy. And, for that reason, something I can cherish.

It can only do you good if you occasionally look forward to and enjoy a delicious dessert. So give your desserts the value they deserve. See them as something extra, something exceptional, something for a special occasion. This way, you will learn to enjoy them even more.

Quinoa with coconut milk and chocolate

WORK: 3 MINUTES - COOKING TIME: 13 MINUTES - SERVES 2

3 1/2 oz quinoa
coconut milk (see tip)
1 1/2 oz bittersweet chocolate (at least 70% cocoa)

Rinse the quinoa thoroughly. Take one part of quinoa to three parts of coconut milk (see tip). Simmer for 13 minutes and then remove from the heat. Stir in the chocolate. Cover with a lid so that the quinoa continues to expand. Serve in small glasses and finish by pouring over a little extra coconut milk.

Tip: quinoa
The normal ratio is one part of quinoa to two parts of liquid, but because we want to make a smooth and creamy pulp and because coconut milk is thicker and more consistent than water, it is better to use three parts for this recipe.

Tip: coconut milk
Coconut milk is made from grated coconut mixed with water. The resulting pulp is stirred thoroughly and the liquid is then pressed out and passed through a strainer. This liquid is coconut milk, and it is as fluid as ordinary milk. Coconut cream contains more of the coconut pulp and is ideal for breakfast, but not for cooking.

Tip: dessert
It tastes like a dessert, so sweet and yet so full of goodness. All three of its ingredients are considered superfoods, which are beneficial for your body. Tasty and healthy really can go hand in hand!

You can eat this for breakfast or as a snack. It tastes like a dessert, but is so yummy and so healthy.

Chocolate mousse on a spiced cookie base

WORK: 30 MINUTES - SERVES 4 TO 6

9 oz spiced ('speculoos' or ginger) cookies
3 oz butter
11 oz chocolate (at least 70% cocoa)
5 eggs
extra chocolate for grating

Melt the butter. Crumble the spiced cookies in a food processor. Mix the melted butter with the cookies and use the resulting mixture to line the bottom and sides of a pie dish. Melt the chocolate in a bain-marie. Separate the egg yolks from the egg whites. Stir the egg yolks firmly into the melted chocolate. Make sure that the chocolate is not warm, so that the egg yolks do not congeal.

Beat the egg whites to a firm peak. Fold gently into the melted chocolate mixture with a spatula.

Pour the chocolate over the biscuit base and decorate with some flakes of grated chocolate. Place in the refrigerator and let set for at least one hour.

Tip: attractive dish
Use an attractive cake dish to make this recipe. It is not simple to serve on plates, and there is a good chance that it will break. For this reason, I prefer to present it directly at table in a nice dish.

Tip: chocolate flakes
You can buy ready-made chocolate flakes in the supermarket. Quick, easy, good to eat and good to look at.

Tip: the day before
You can make this dish one day ahead.

Like every dessert should be: just too delicious for words!

Pear and ginger cake

WORK: 20 MINUTES · COOKING TIME: 40 MINUTES · SERVES 4

3 eggs
3 pears
4 oz coconut sugar (or
 ordinary sugar)
5 ½ oz whole wheat flour
3 ½ oz olive oil
3 to 4 tablespoons of
 grated ginger

Preheat the oven to 350°F.
Beat together the eggs, flour, sugar and olive oil into a smooth mixture. Stir in the grated ginger. Pour this dough into a pie dish. Halve and peel the pears, removing the cores. Place them in the dough, with the convex side on top.
Put the dish in the oven and bake for 35 to 40 minutes.

Tip: coconut sugar
This sweetener is well-known and often used in oriental countries. It is made from the nectar of the coconut flower. Incisions are made in the leaves of the flowers and pots are hung underneath to collect the dripping nectar. This work is carried out by the so-called 'tappers', who climb high into the palm trees without the use of ladders.

Nobody can resist the temptation of this cakes warm and sweet aroma.

Fruit tart with ricotta

WORK: 30 MINUTES - TIME IN REFRIGERATOR: 30 MINUTES - COOKING TIME: 30 MINUTES - SERVES 6

6 oz ricotta
6 tablespoons of liquid honey
apples
blueberries

FOR THE PASTRY:
9 oz flour
6 oz butter
2½ oz coconut sugar (or ordinary sugar)
2 tablespoons of water
1 egg white

First, make the pastry. Put the flour, sugar and water in a bowl. Cut the butter into small pieces and add to the bowl. Knead everything firmly (roll up your sleeves!) until you have a nice, uniform dough. Roll the dough into a ball and wrap it in plastic film. Place in the refrigerator for 30 minutes, although making sure that the butter in the dough does not become hard again.

In the meantime, stir together the ricotta and 3 tablespoons of the liquid honey. Peel the apples and cut them into thin slices. Sprinkle a cookie sheet with flour. Roll out the dough onto the cookie sheet. Don't worry if it cracks easily. Just put the cracked edges against each other and press them gently together with your fingers.

Preheat the oven to 350°F.

Spread a thick layer of ricotta on top of the pastry dough, to within 2 inches of the edge. Arrange the fruit (apple slices and blueberries) on top of the ricotta and cover with the remaining 3 tablespoons of honey. Fold the edge of the pastry dough over the fruit. Again, don't worry if the pastry cracks; short crust pastry always cracks. Just press the cracked edges back together with your fingers. It doesn't need to look like a work of art; rough-and-ready will do just fine! This gives the tart its character. Brush egg white over the dough, so that it will turn golden brown when baked.

Bake for 25 to 30 minutes.

Serve either hot or cold.

Tip: nectarines or sweet plums
During the summer this fruit tart is also yummy with nectarines and blueberries, or with sweet plums.

But surely we are all living longer? Yes, we are — but don't be fooled. We are sick for more than half of our lives. Our profit comes from the number of healthy years we can enjoy.

Fast carbohydrates

BREAD, PASTA AND POTATOES HAVE BECOME BAD FOR US...

What are carbohydrates?
Carbohydrates include things like fruit and vegetables, fibers, alcohol and starch. Slow carbohydrates, such as fruit and vegetables, are healthy because they release their sugars slowly. Fast carbohydrates are unhealthy, because they can cause high sugar spikes. What are fast carbohydrates? Sugar, white bread, cookies, cakes, potatoes, white rice, breakfast cereals, soft drinks, processed fruit juices, etc.

Why are fast carbohydrates so bad for us? This is related to:
- The quantity of carbohydrates we eat nowadays.
- The gluten contained in cereals.
- The speed with which the sugars from carbohydrates are deposited in our body.

The quantity[1]
We can only store a limited amount of carbohydrates in our body: about 200 grams in our muscles and between 100 and 150 grams in our liver. Most people eat around 500 grams of carbohydrate each day. If the storage capacity of the muscles and liver is full, the excess carbohydrates are converted and stored as fat. So if you eat too many carbohydrates, whether you are healthy or not, your liver will make more and more fat. What's worse, it is primarily saturated fat.

Gluten[2]
Cereals contain gluten. This protein is broken down in our intestines into smaller proteins. These can sometimes provoke a reaction, so that our immune system targets our own body. A large part of the population in Western societies suffers from this autoimmune reaction, known as celiac disease. This disease is responsible for stomach and intestinal disorders in 1 out of every 6 sufferers. In addition, many others are over-sensitive for the effects of cereals.

Speed [3]

The speed with which sugars find their way into your blood is an important health factor. If you eat fast carbohydrates, the glucose level in your blood rises quickly, so that your body reacts to counterbalance this undesired effect. In particular, your pancreas will produce extra insulin to nullify the glucose spike. And so your insulin levels rise as well - and this is the real problem. If you eat lots of fast sugars, your insulin levels are constantly high, and this significantly increases your risk of cardiovascular disease. Worse still, once all the sugars are absorbed, the sugar outflow from your intestines stops suddenly. Consequently, your blood sugar levels fall dramatically, while your insulin levels still remain high. This is known as hypoglycemia. You feel faint and sleepy, and you suddenly feel hungry again. In other words, you have eaten a huge amount of energy in the form of sugar, but within a short period of time you end up feeling hungry again! And so the vicious circle continues.

"Throughout recent history we have replaced fruit and vegetables with highly processed, carbohydrate-rich foods. We now urgently need to move back toward fruit and vegetables."

PROF. F.A.J. MUSKIET

How do I get my carbohydrates?

I never buy bread, potatoes, pasta or rice. I get all my carbohydrates from fruit and vegetables. This is more than adequate, and I can assure you that I have more than enough energy!

Do I never eat pasta or French fries?

Yes, I occasionally allow myself to be tempted. After all, French fries are really yummy. But I soon pay the price. Immediately after the meal I feel sluggish and tired. My stomach protests loudly, I can't sleep when I go to bed that night and when I step on the scale the next morning I know I will have put on weight. If I eat the same amount, or even more, of the right food combinations - in other words, fish or meat with just vegetables - then I feel full of energy and my weight will remain stable. I try to make my dishes so tasty that I won't miss my French fries. And it works. At home, I never have a craving for French fries. I simply prefer my own food.

[1] [2] [3] This explanation was provided by Professor Muskiet during my interview with him in February 2013 for the magazine *Vitaya*.

My desire for simplicty and beauty

I try to make the world a more beautiful place, both from the inside and the outside. How you eat is just as important as what you eat. Eating your food at an attractive table in enjoyable company will certainly give you a feeling of greater satisfaction, but also a feeling of greater respect for the food itself. Personally, I love simple, elegant and authentic forms. They give off such strength! In my desire to create my own world, I discovered the unique possibilities offered by the centuries' old craft of pottery. My biggest source of inspiration is nature. In fact, I want to stay close to nature in everything that I do. This way, I feel that I am being true to myself. My pottery work shows the unmistakable signs of natural processes and my pieces are certainly not technically perfect. But they are each unique, and therefore perfect in their very imperfection. This is the strength that they exude. Nothing in nature is perfect. Not you, not me, not the tree in my garden, and not the pottery I make. It is precisely this that makes them unique, according to the Japanese Wabi Sabi philosophy. I would recommend everyone to try and express his or her creativity. Go in search of what you want. Develop your talents. Create your own world. Anyone can do it. I never thought that I was creative, until I finally discovered myself. And now look at the result! My thanks go to my pottery teacher, Bie van Gucht: a truly inspirational woman in more ways than one.

PURE
by
PASCALE NAESSENS

for
SERAX
TABLEWARE

I make the plates, the crockery and the recipes. Cooking delicious food in beautiful ceramics is pure romance and pure communication.

My newest collection for 'Pure' is my range of oven dishes.

Index of recipes

Index of ingredients

www.lannoo.com

Register on our website and we will send you a regular newsletter with information about new books and interesting, exclusive offers.

www.purepascale.com

Recipes, texts, styling, design concept: Pascale Naessens

Photography:

Heikki Verdurme: pages 1, 31, 32, 33, 37, 39, 41, 45, 47, 48, 49, 52, 53, 55, 57, 59, 61, 69, 71,73, 75, 77, 85, 87, 93, 95, 99, 102, 103, 105, 107, 109, 110, 111, 113, 115, 118, 119, 120, 121, 123, 125, 127, 129, 133, 135, 137, 139, 140, 141, 147, 149, 151, 153, 155, 157, 159, 165, 167, 168, 169, 171, 173, 175, 177, 187

Diego Franssens: cover, inside cover and pages 2, 3, 4, 5, 8, 10, 18, 19, 24, 25, 27, 30, 64, 65, 66, 67, 78, 79, 81, 83, 91, 100, 101, 131, 142, 143, 181, 184, 185, 186, 188, 191

Wout Hendrickx: pages 35, 43, 51, 63, 89, 97, 116, 117, 144, 145, 161, 163

Layout: Whitespray

English translation: Ian Connerty

If you have any comments or questions, you can contact our editorial team at: redactielifestyle@lannoo.com

© Lannoo Publishers, Tielt-Belgium, 2014
D/2014/45/534 – NUR 440-441
ISBN: 978 94 014 1983 3